ILLUMINATION PRESENTS
Dr. Seuss'
The GRINCH

ISBN: 978-1-5400-4515-7

HAL•LEONARD®

Visit Hal Leonard Online at
www.halleonard.com

Contact us:
Hal Leonard
7777 West Bluemound Road
Milwaukee, WI 53213
Email: info@halleonard.com

In Europe, contact:
Hal Leonard Europe Limited
42 Wigmore Street
Marylebone, London, W1U 2RY
Email: info@halleonardeurope.com

In Australia, contact:
Hal Leonard Australia Pty. Ltd.
4 Lentara Court
Cheltenham, Victoria, 3192 Australia
Email: info@halleonard.com.au

CONTENTS

YOU'RE A MEAN ONE, MR. GRINCH

Lyrics by DR. SEUSS
Music by ALBERT HAGUE

* *Recorded half a step lower.*

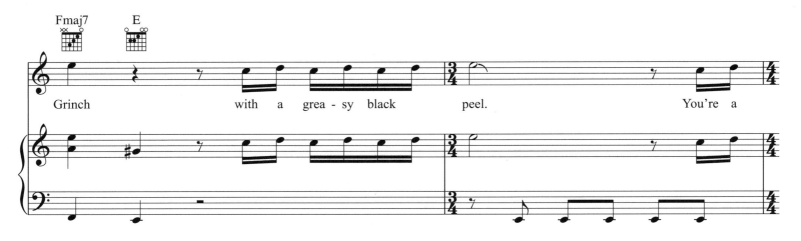

Grinch with a grea-sy black peel. You're a

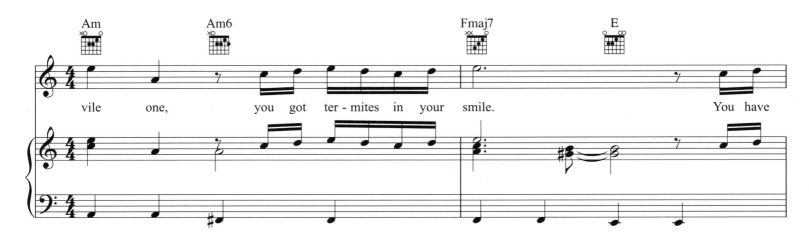

vile one, you got ter-mites in your smile. You have

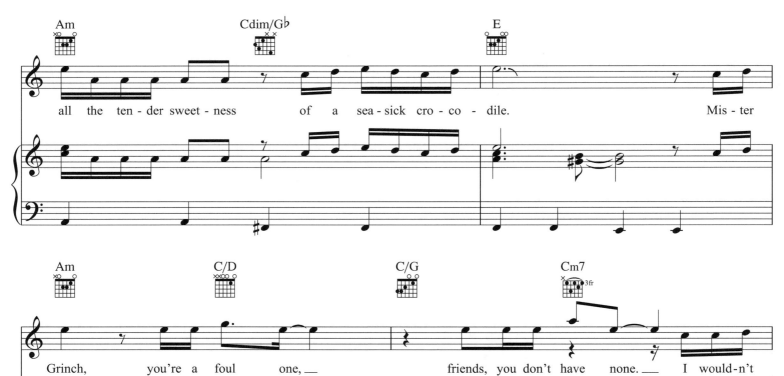

all the ten-der sweet-ness of a sea-sick cro-co-dile. Mis-ter

Grinch, you're a foul one, __ friends, you don't have none. __ I would-n't

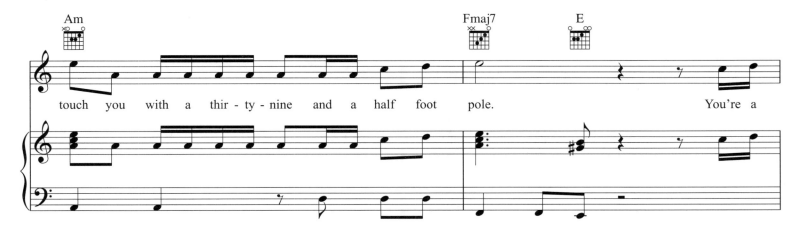

touch you with a thir-ty-nine and a half foot pole. You're a

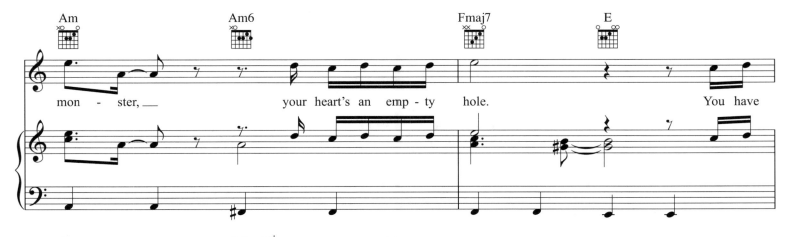

mon - ster, ___ your heart's an emp-ty hole. You have

gar - lic in your soul.
You got gar - lic, you got gar - lic in your soul.

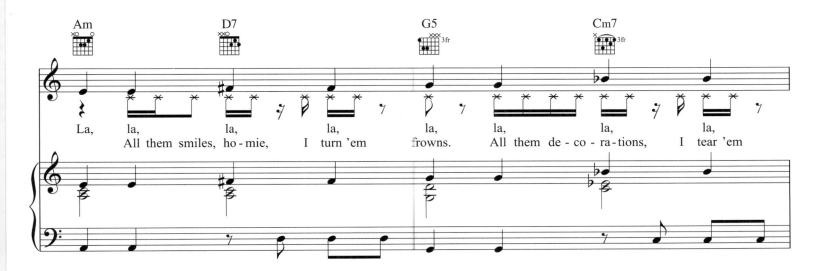

La, la, la, la, la, la, la,
All them smiles, ho-mie, I turn 'em frowns. All them de-co-ra-tions, I tear 'em

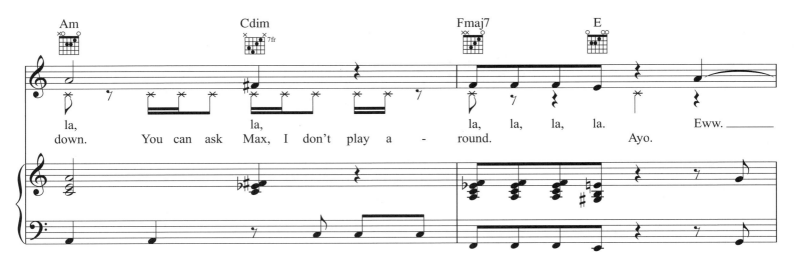

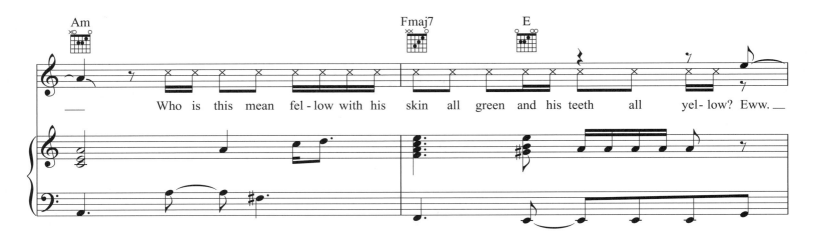

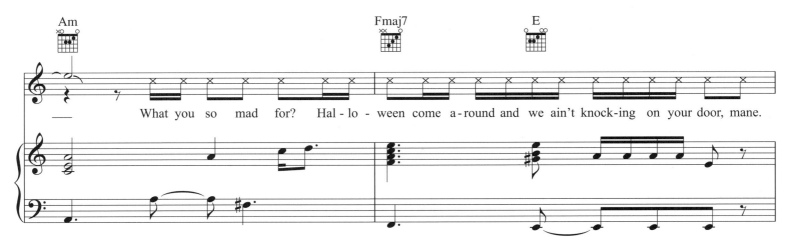

I AM THE GRINCH

Words and Music by TYLER OKONMA

Laid-back

N.C.

Drum groove

E7sus — Amaj9

I am the Grinch, Cin-dy Lou who? I live in Who - ville, who are you? I got a

E7sus — Amaj9

dog, his name is Max. Coffee in my cup, that is a fact. I was in

E7sus — Amaj9

snow, ain't need no coat, max with the sled, off with their head. I don't like

I am the Grinch. That's what they call me when they talk a-bout me a-round the
love. _____

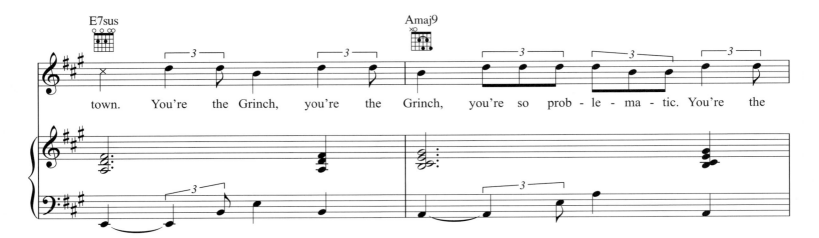

town. You're the Grinch, you're the Grinch, you're so prob - le - ma - tic. You're the

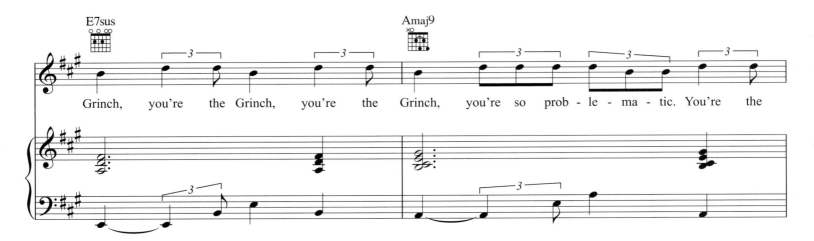

Grinch, you're the Grinch, you're the Grinch, you're so prob - le - ma - tic. You're the

Grinch, you're the rinch, you're the Grinch, you're so prob - le - ma - tic. You're the

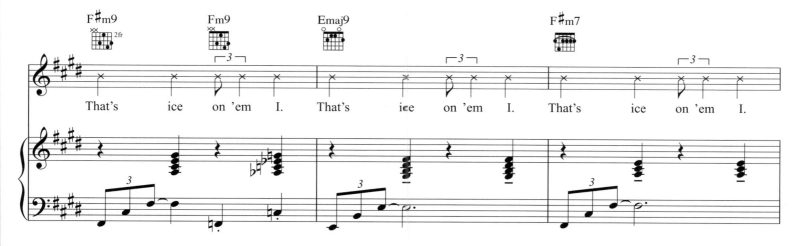

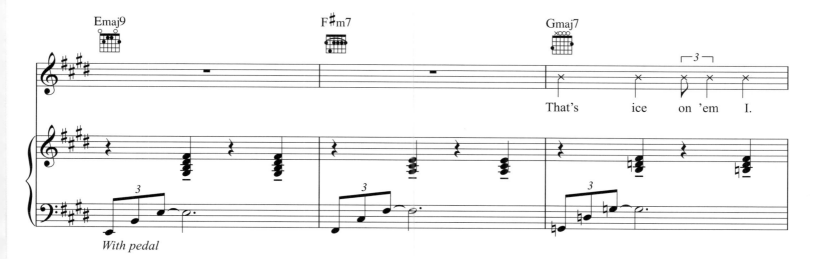

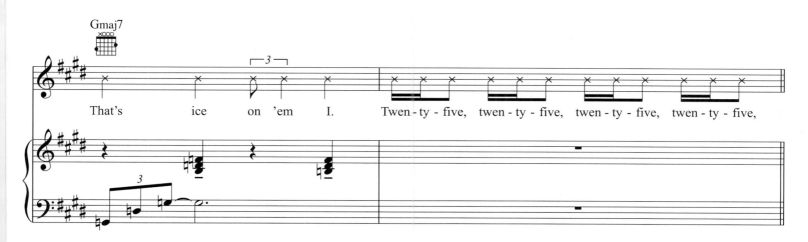

twen-ty-five days in a month, twen-ty-five days ain't e-nough where I don't give a. (Wait a min-ute.)

Twen-ty-five days got the lock with the chain at the door, don't knock, no gifts o-ver here.

I don't smell noth-ing in the air, you can take that o-ver there and I don't real-ly care. Tell your

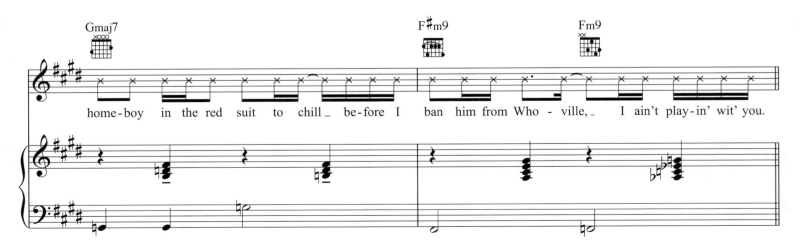

home-boy in the red suit to chill _ be-fore I ban him from Who - ville, _ I ain't play-in' wit' you.

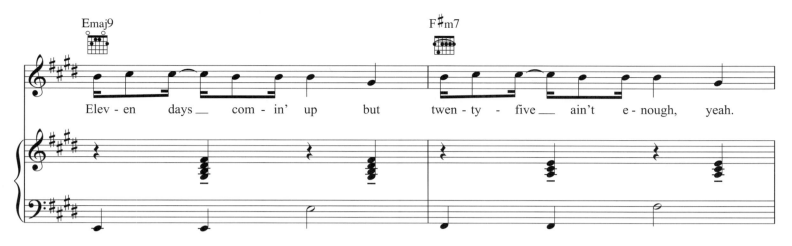

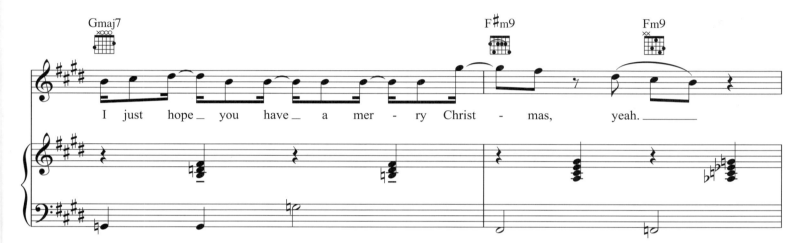

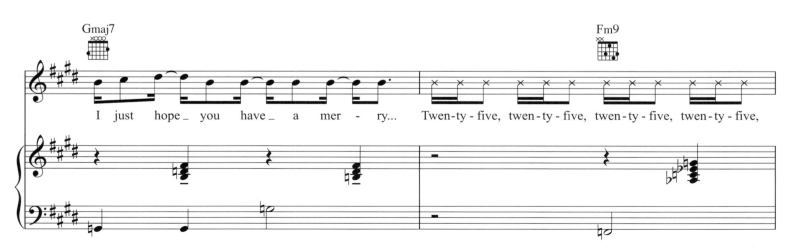

CHRISTMAS IS

Words and Music by DARRYL McDANIELS
and JOSEPH SIMMONS

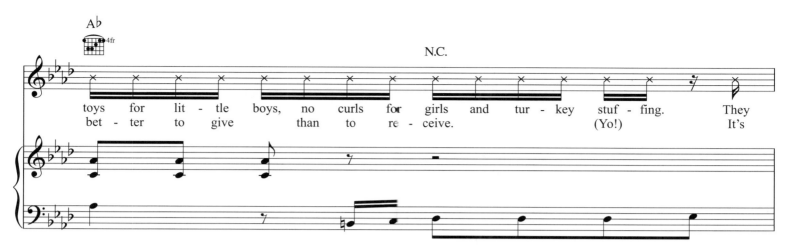

toys for lit - tle boys, no curls for girls and tur - key stuf - fing. They
bet - ter to give than to re - ceive. (Yo!) It's

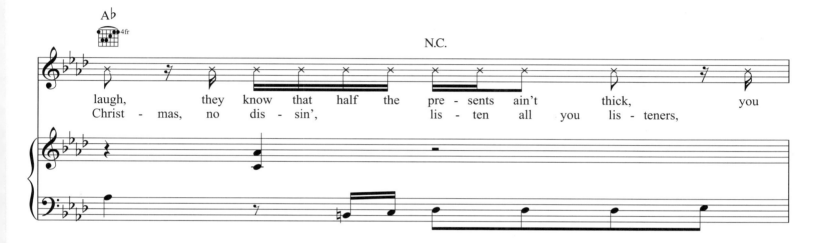

laugh, they know that half the pre - sents ain't thick, you
Christ - mas, no dis - sin', lis - ten all you lis - teners,

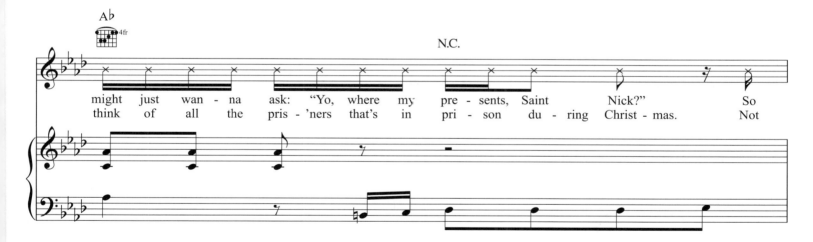

might just wan - na ask: "Yo, where my pre - sents, Saint Nick?" So
think of all the pris - 'ners that's in pri - son du - ring Christ - mas. Not

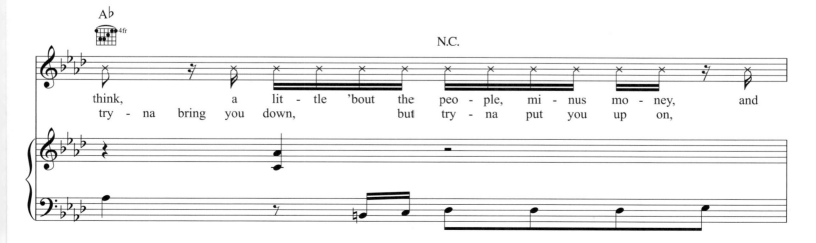

think, a lit - tle 'bout the peo - ple, mi - nus mo - ney, and
try - na bring you down, but try - na put you up on,

when you get your dough, why don't you show some kind-ness, ho-ney? Go
lan-ded on the ta-ble so you're a-ble to put your cup on. No

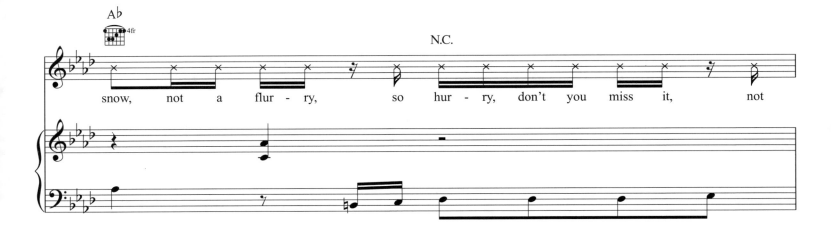

snow, not a flur-ry, so hur-ry, don't you miss it, not

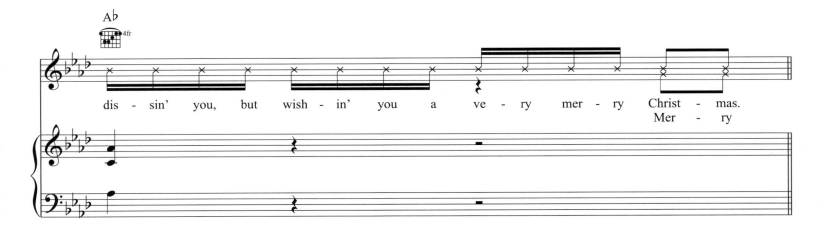

dis-sin' you, but wish-in' you a ve-ry mer-ry Christ-mas. Mer-ry

Give up the dough! Give up the dough! Give up the dough on Christ-mas, yo!
Christ-mas! Mer-ry

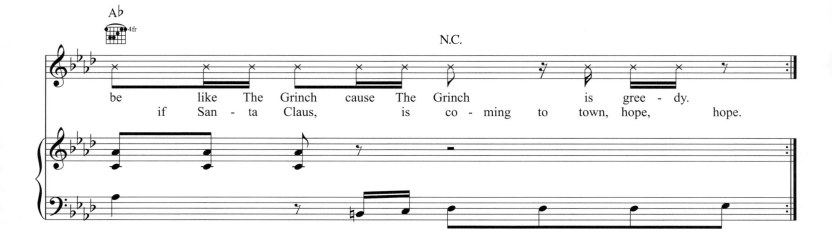

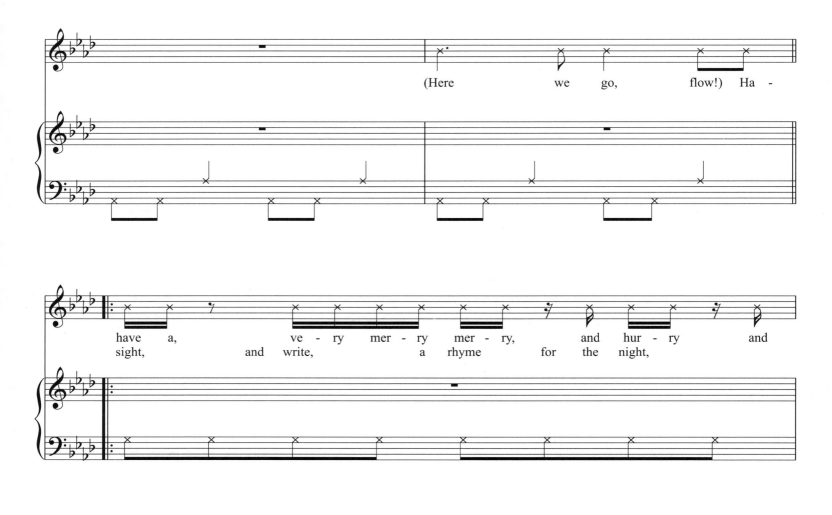

(Here we go, flow!) Ha -

have a, ve - ry mer - ry mer - ry, and hur - ry and
sight, and write, a rhyme for the night,

if you'll need a lea - der, run - 'll be there for your blur - ry, blur - ry
Christ - mas is the time for giv - ing not for the type. So

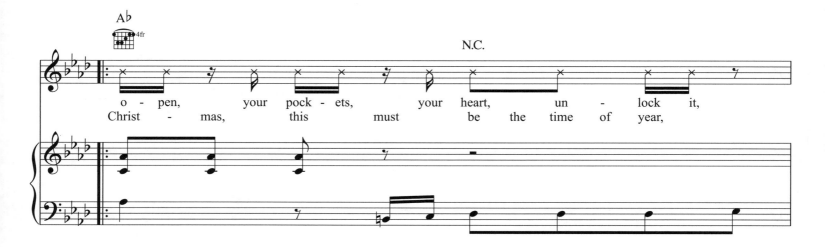

o - pen, your pock - ets, your heart, un - lock it,
Christ - mas, this must be the time of year,

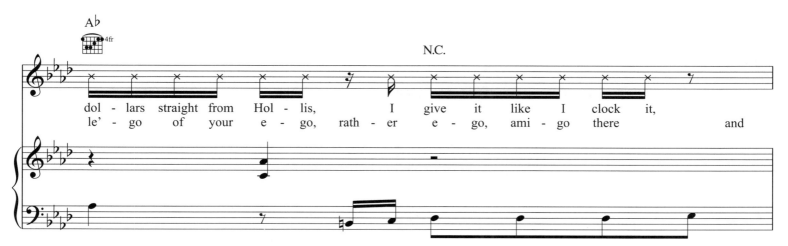

dol - lars straight from Hol - lis, I give it like I clock it,
le' - go of your e - go, rath - er e - go, ami - go there and

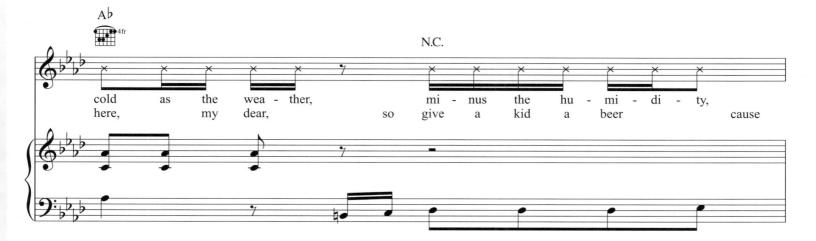

cold as the wea - ther, mi - nus the hu - mi - di - ty,
here, my dear, so give a kid a beer cause

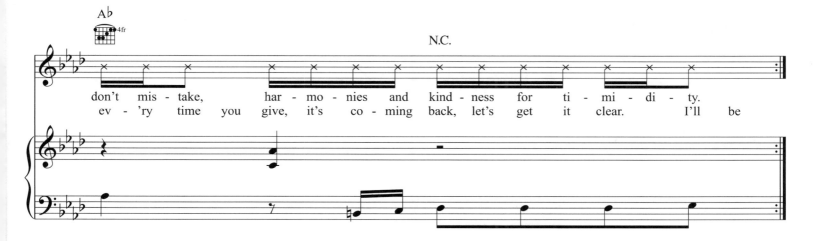

don't mis - take, har - mo - nies and kind - ness for ti - mi - di - ty.
ev - 'ry time you give, it's co - ming back, let's get it clear. I'll be

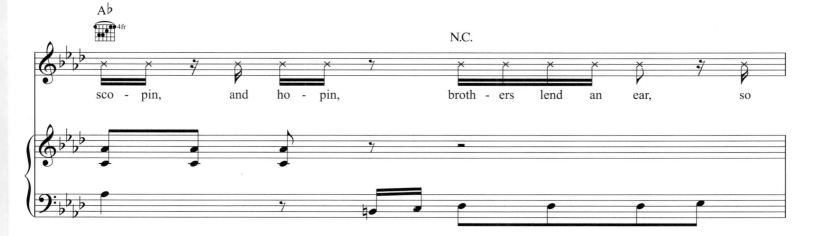

sco - pin, and ho - pin, broth - ers lend an ear, so

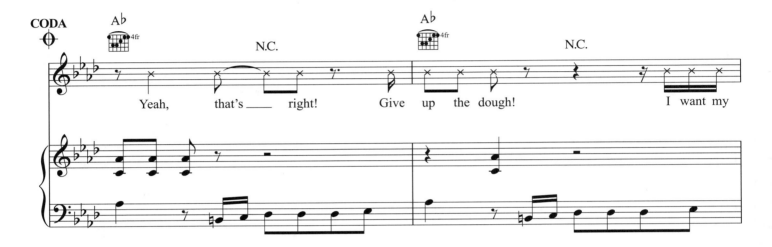

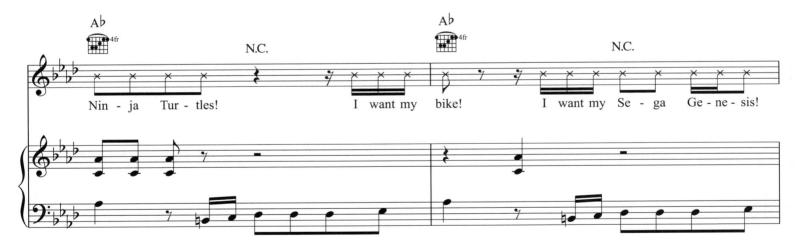

DECK THE HALLS

Traditional
Arranged by JOHNNY MICHAELS
and NAT TARNOPOL

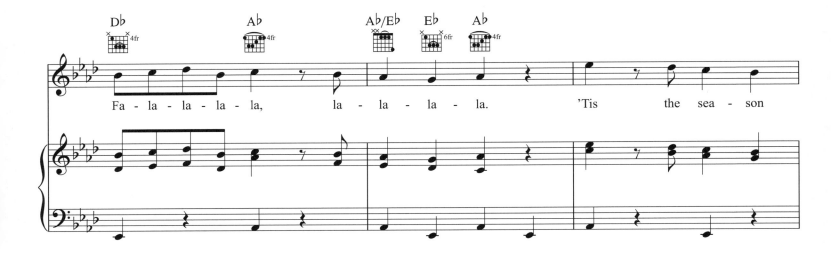

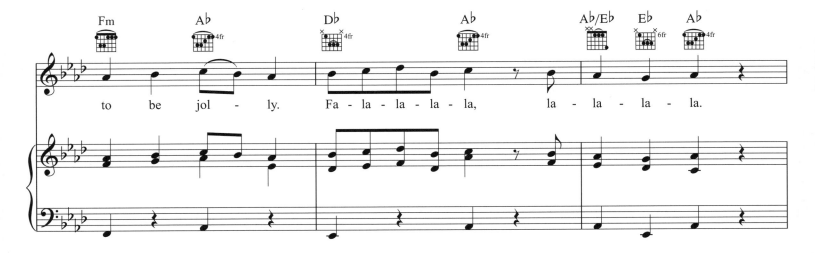

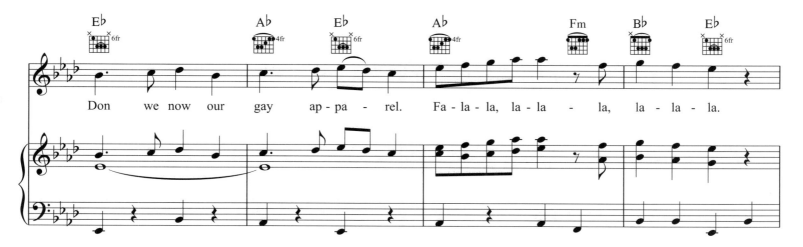

Don we now our gay ap-pa-rel. Fa-la-la, la-la-la, la-la-la.

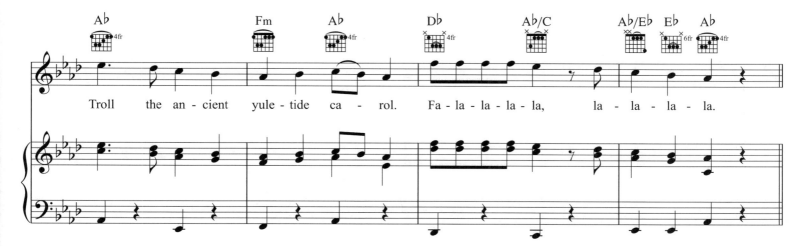

Troll the an-cient yule-tide ca-rol. Fa-la-la-la-la, la-la-la-la.

See the bla-zing yule be-fore __ us. Fa-la-la-la-la, la-la-la-la.

Strike the harp and join the cho-rus. Fa-la-la-la-la, la-

la - la - la - la. Fol - low me in mer - ry mea - sure.

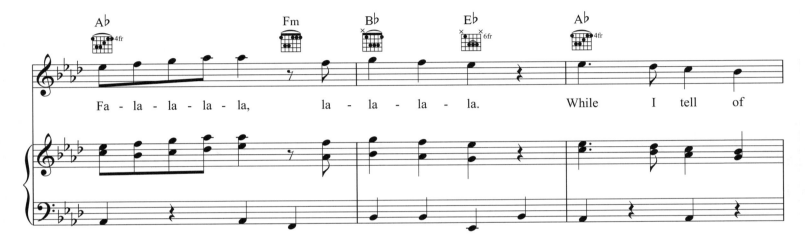

Fa - la - la - la - la, la - la - la - la. While I tell of

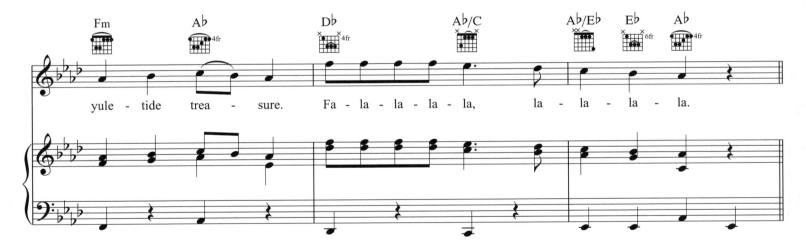

yule - tide trea - sure. Fa - la - la - la - la, la - la - la - la.

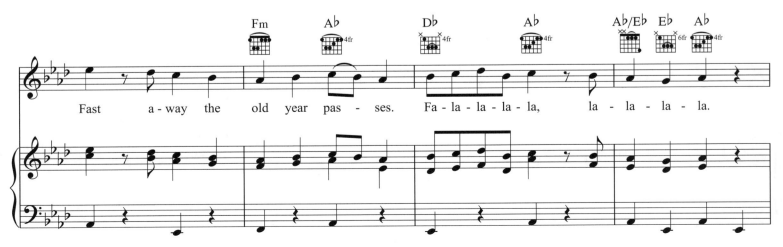

Fast a - way the old year pas - ses. Fa - la - la - la - la, la - la - la - la.

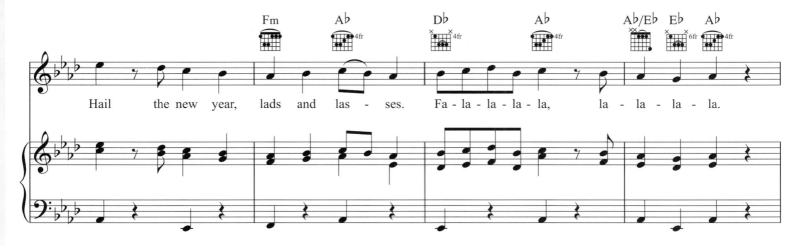

Hail the new year, lads and las - ses. Fa - la - la - la - la, la - la - la - la.

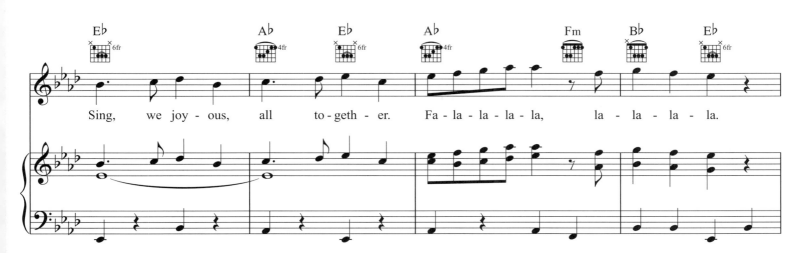

Sing, we joy - ous, all to - geth - er. Fa - la - la - la - la, la - la - la - la.

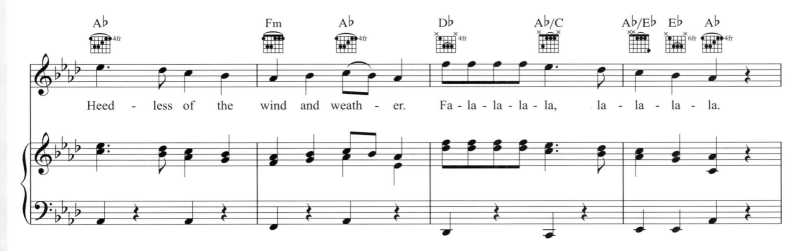

Heed - less of the wind and weath - er. Fa - la - la - la - la, la - la - la - la.

Sing, we joy - ous, all to - geth - er. Fa - la - la - la - la, la - la - la - la.

RUN RUDOLPH RUN

Music and Lyrics by JOHNNY MARKS
and MARVIN BRODIE

Out _____ of all the rein - deers, you know you're the mas - ter - mind. _

Run, _____ run, Ru - dolph,

Ran - dolph ain't too far be - hind. _____ Run, _

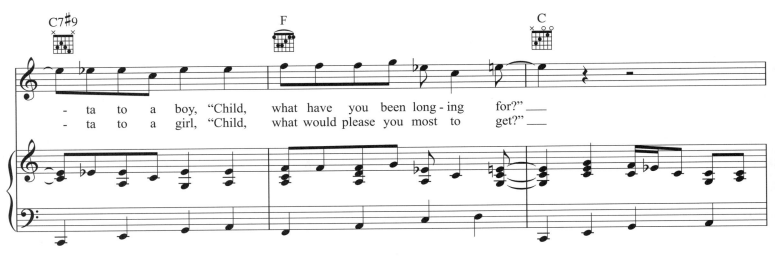

- ta to a boy, "Child, what have you been long-ing for?" ___
- ta to a girl, "Child, what would please you most to get?" ___

"All ___ I want for Christ-mas is a rock 'n' roll e - lec-tric gui-tar." ___
"A lit-tle ba-by doll ___ that can cry, ___ sleep, ___ drink and wet." ___

___ And then a - way went Ru - dolph,
And then a - way went Ru - dolph,

whiz-zin' like a shoot-ing star. ___
whiz-zin' like a Sab - er jet. ___

Yeah, } run, ___
Oh, }

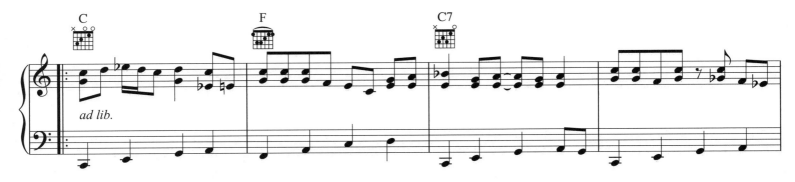

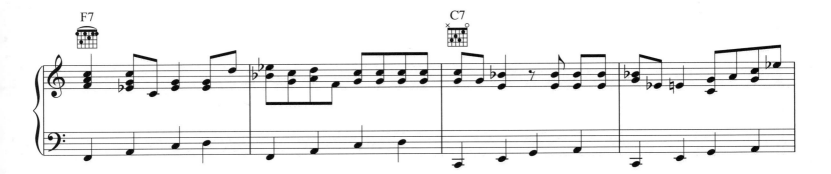

MY FAVORITE THINGS

Lyrics by OSCAR HAMMERSTEIN II
Music by RICHARD RODGERS

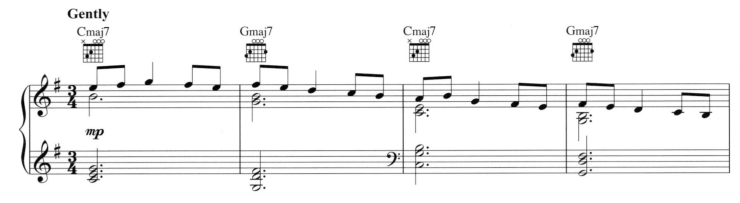

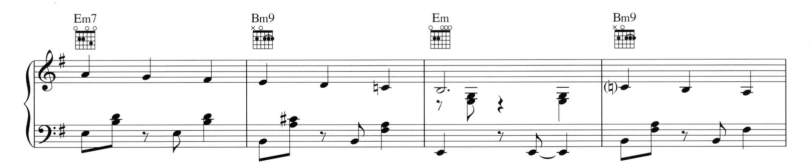

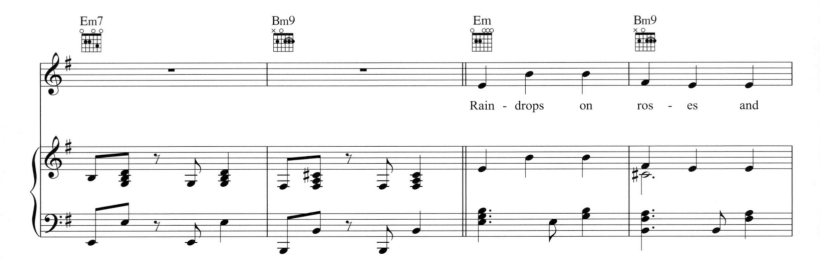

Rain - drops on ros - es and

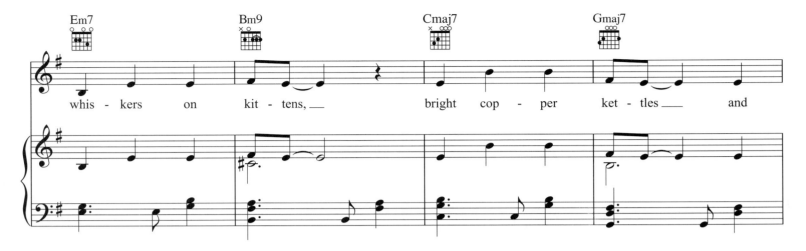

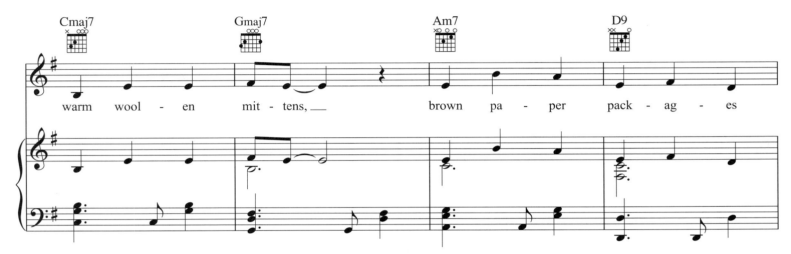

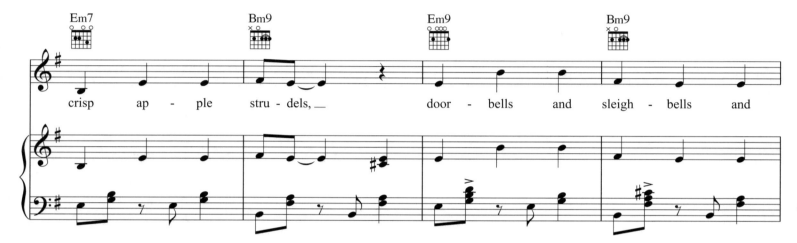

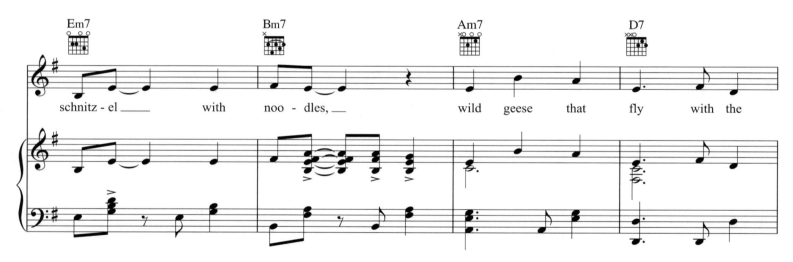

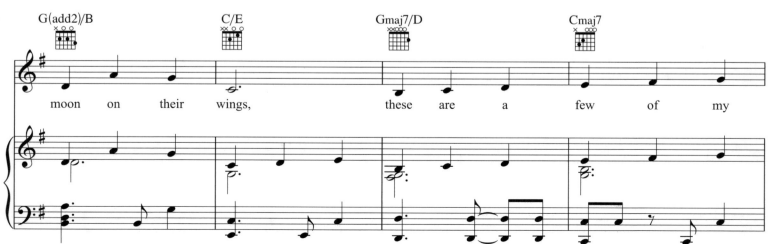

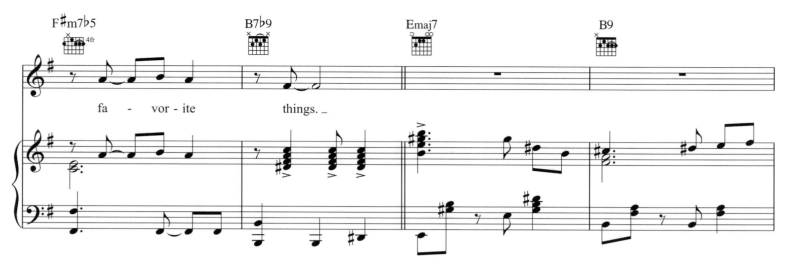

fa - vor - ite things. _

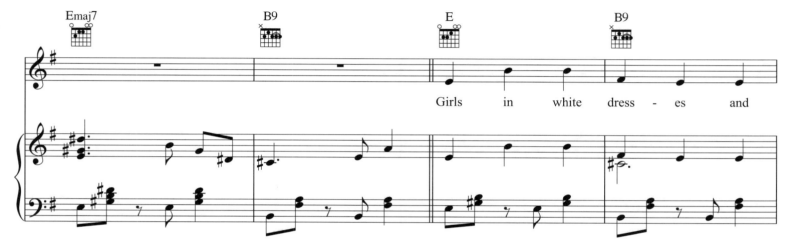

Girls in white dress - es and

blue sat - in sash - es, ___ snow - flakes that stay on ___ my

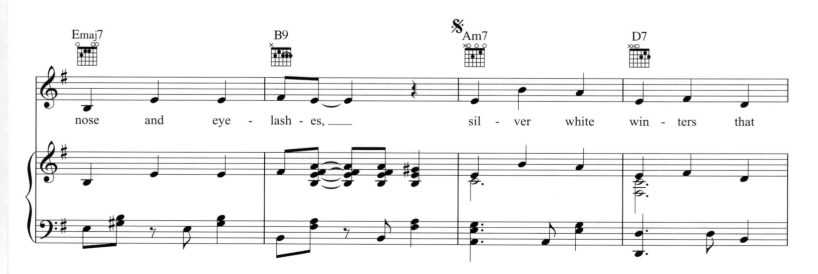

nose and eye - lash - es, ___ sil - ver white win - ters that

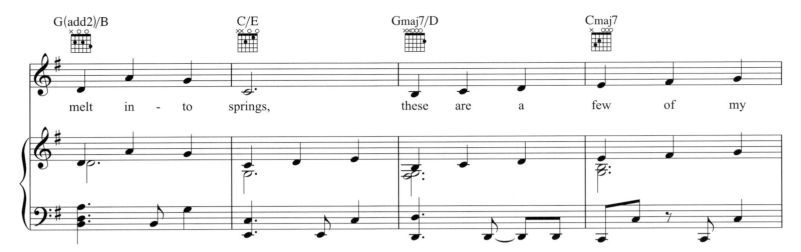

melt in - to springs, these are a few of my

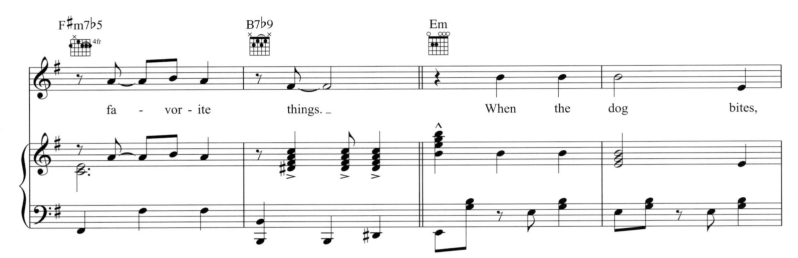

fa - vor - ite things. ___ When the dog bites,

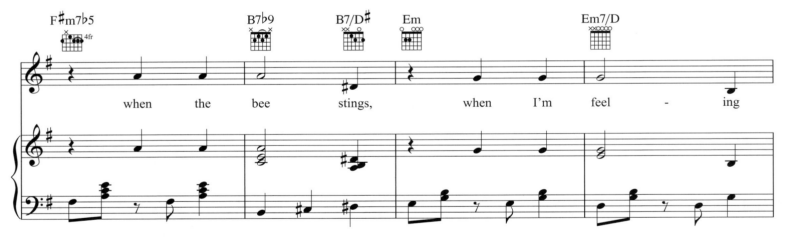

when the bee stings, when I'm feel - ing

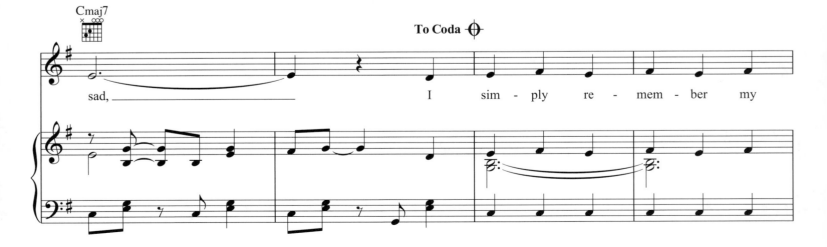

To Coda ⊕

sad, _____ I sim - ply re - mem - ber my

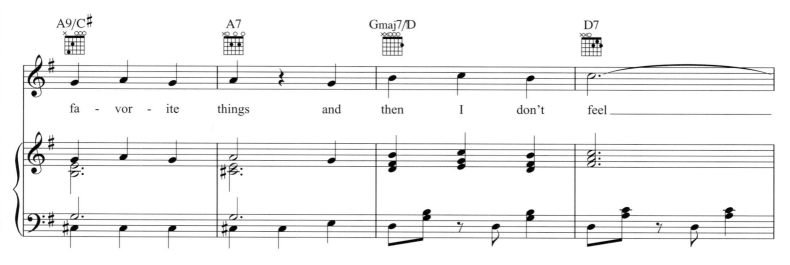

fa - vor - ite   things   and   then   I   don't   feel _____

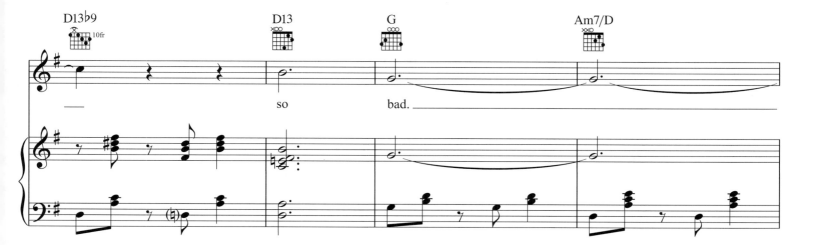

_____   so   bad. _____

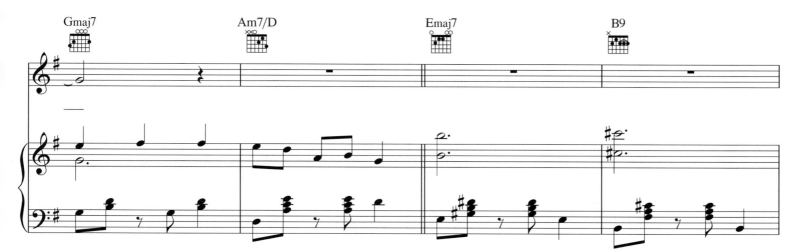

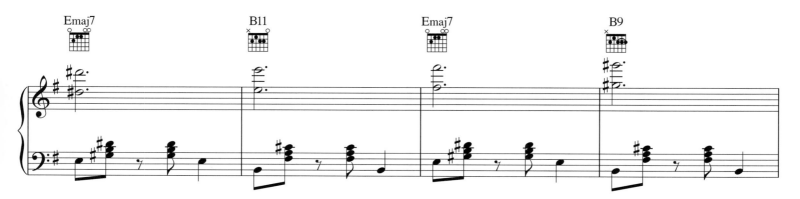

48

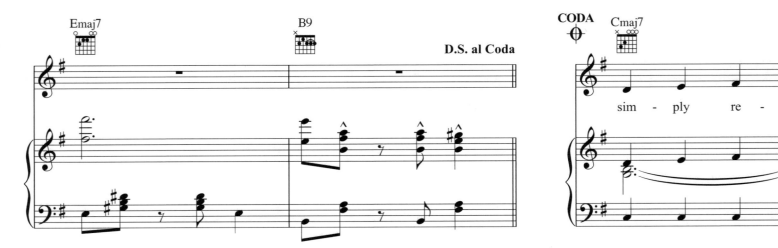

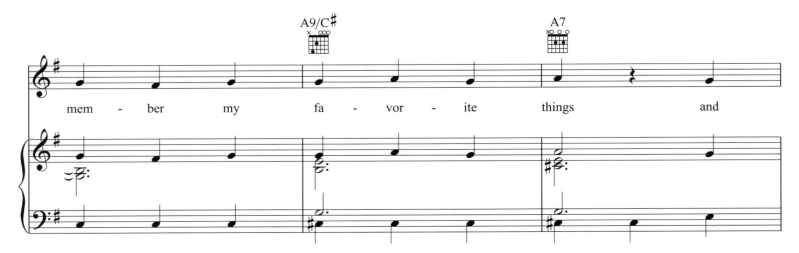

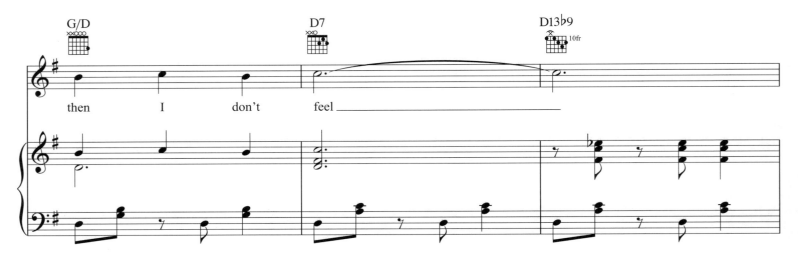

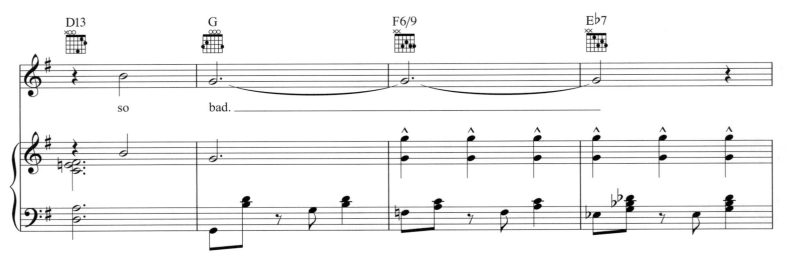

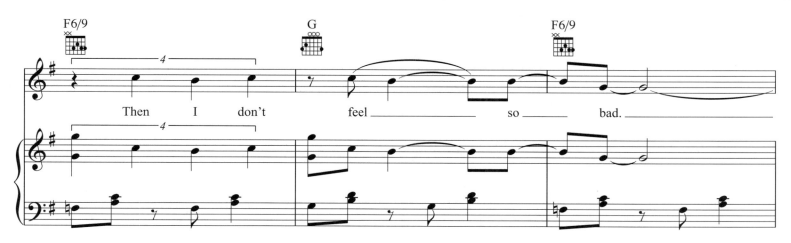

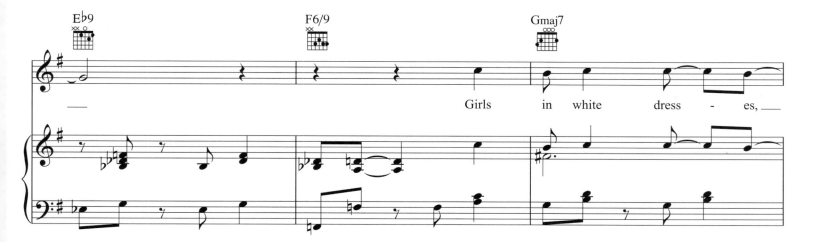

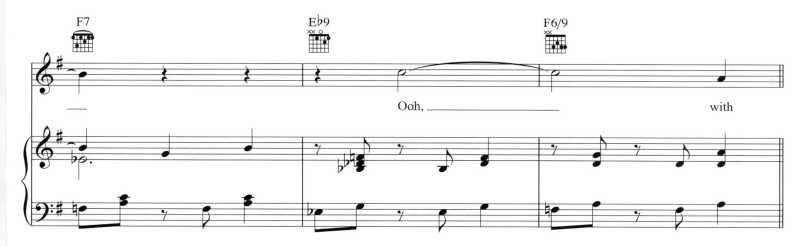

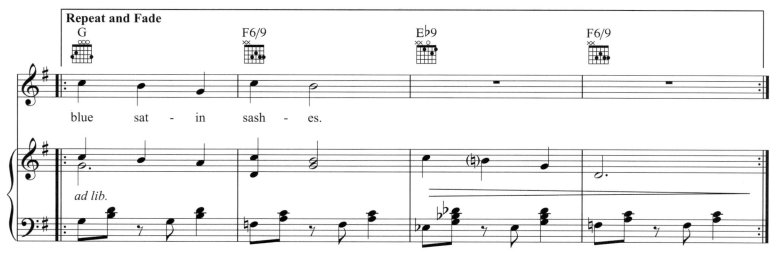

'ZAT YOU, SANTA CLAUS?

Words and Music by JACK FOX

Moderate Swing

Gifts I'm pre-par-in' for some Christ-mas shar-in', but I pause be-cause hang-in' my stock-in', I can hear a knock-in'. 'Zat you, __ San-ta Claus? __

Is that you, __ San - ta Claus? __

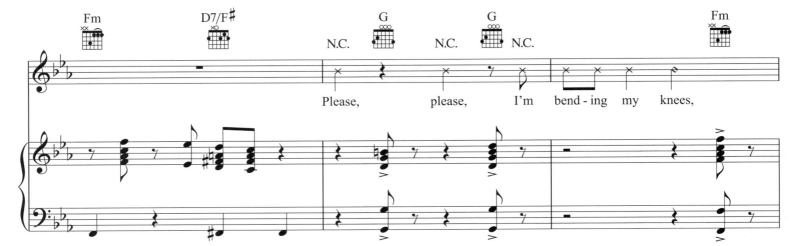

Please, please, I'm bend-ing my knees,

is that you, __ San - ta Claus? _____

That's him alright.

CHRISTMAS IN HOLLIS

Words and Music by DARRYL McDANIELS,
JASON MIZELL and JOSEPH SIMMONS

Moderate Hip-Hop

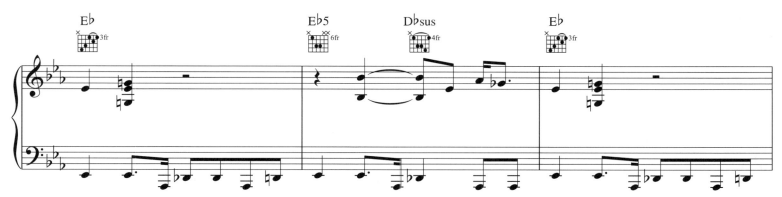

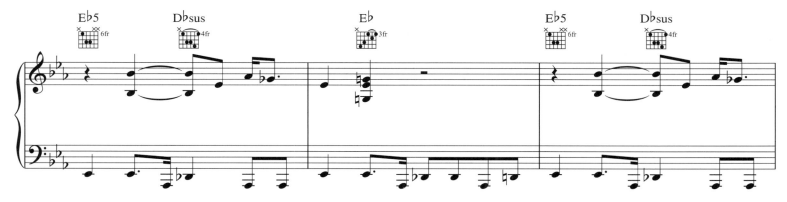

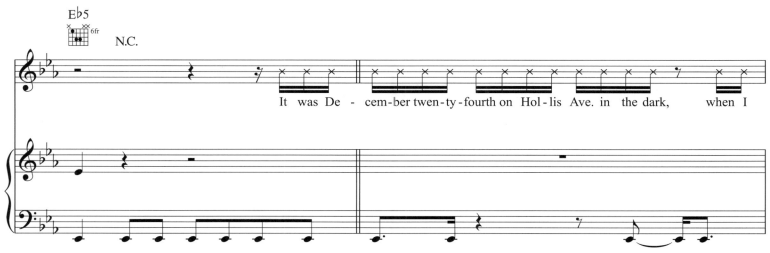

It was De - cem-ber twen-ty-fourth on Hol-lis Ave. in the dark, when I

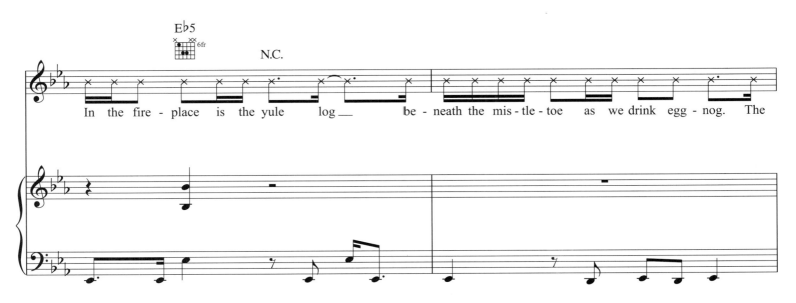

In the fire - place is the yule log __ be - neath the mis - tle - toe as we drink egg - nog. The

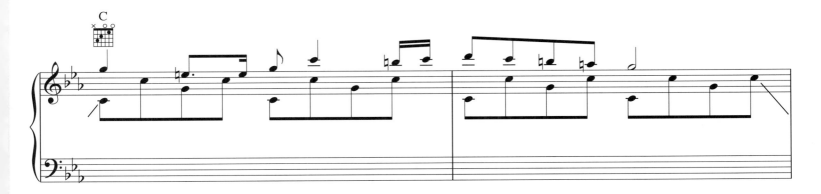

rhymes that you hear are the rhymes of Dar - ryl's, but each and ev - 'ry year we bust Christ - mas car - ols.

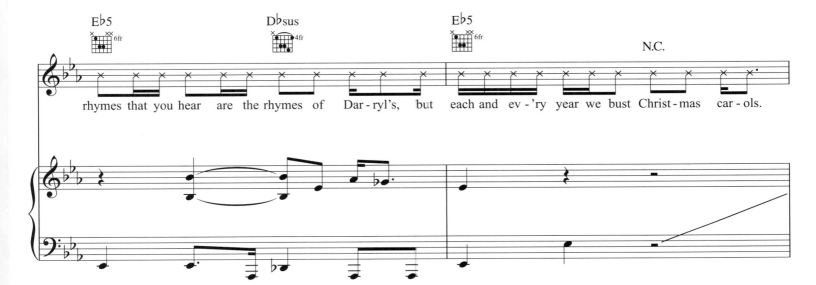

JINGLE BELLS

Words and Music by JAMES PIERPONT
Arranged by BRIAN SETZER

Rock Shuffle

Jin - gle bells, _ jin - gle bells, _ jin - gle all the way, _

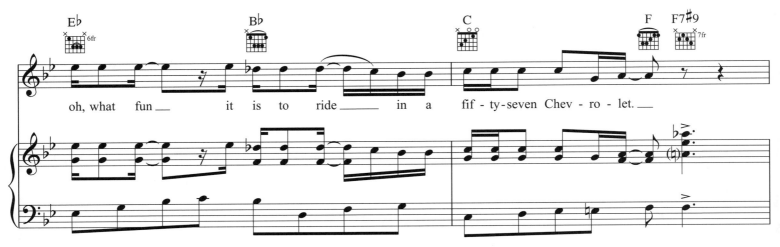

oh, what fun _ it is to ride _____ in a fif - ty-seven Chev - ro - let. _

Jin - gle bells, _ jin - gle jin - gle, jin - gle all the way, _

oh, what fun __ it is to ride _____ in a one-horse o - pen sleigh.

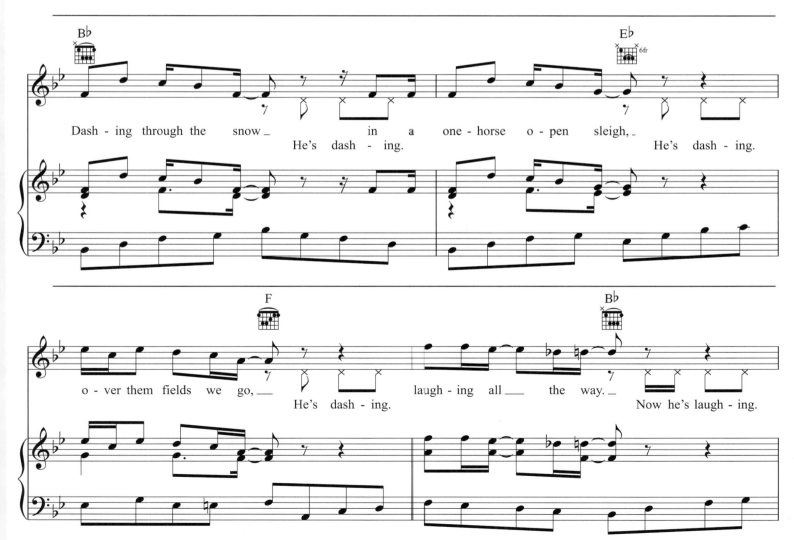

Dash - ing through the snow _ in a one - horse o - pen sleigh, _
He's dash - ing. He's dash - ing.

o - ver them fields we go, __ laugh - ing all __ the way. _
He's dash - ing. Now he's laugh - ing.

Bells on bob tails ring, making them spi - rits bright, _ what

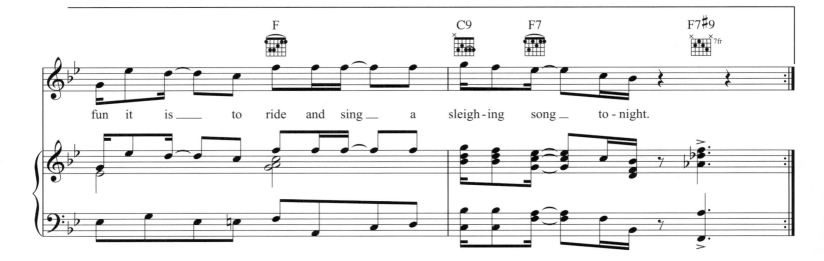

fun it is ___ to ride and sing ___ a sleigh-ing song ___ to - night.

one-horse o - pen sleigh.

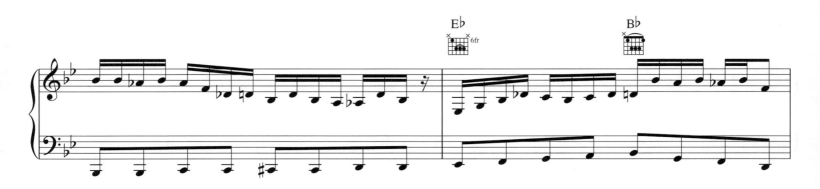

Dash - ing through the snow _ in a

one - horse o - pen sleigh, _   o - ver them fields we go, _   laugh -

ing, laugh - ing, __ laugh - ing, __ laugh - ing, __ laugh - ing. Bells on bob tails ring,

mak - ing them spi - rits bright, __ what fun it is __ to ride and sing __ a

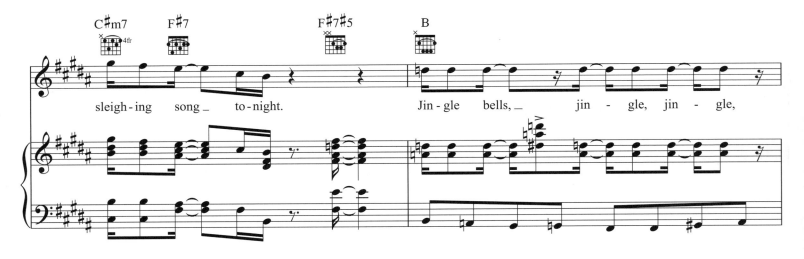

sleigh - ing song __ to - night. Jin - gle bells, __ jin - gle, jin - gle,

jin - gle all the way, __ oh, what fun it is to ride __ in a

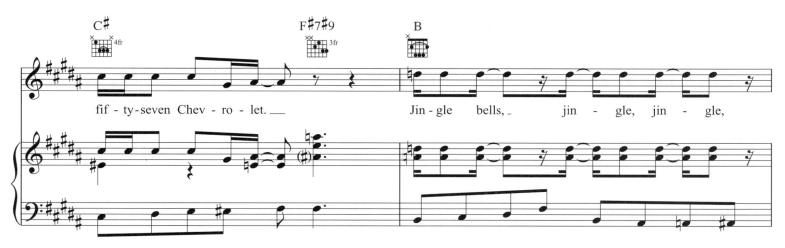

fif - ty-seven Chev - ro - let. ___ Jin - gle bells, ___ jin - gle, jin - gle,

jin - gle all the way, ___ oh, what fun ___ it is to ride ___ in a

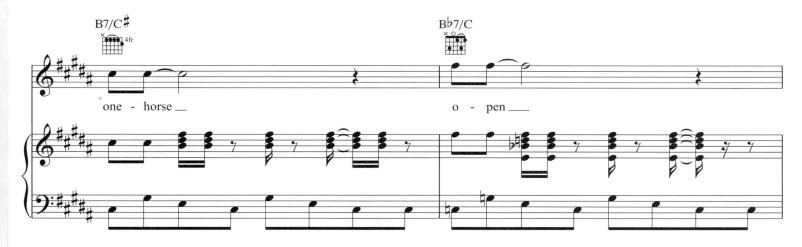

one - horse ___ o - pen ___

sleigh. _____

THE CHRISTMAS SONG
(CHESTNUTS ROASTING ON AN OPEN FIRE)

Music and Lyrics by MEL TORME
and ROBERT WELLS

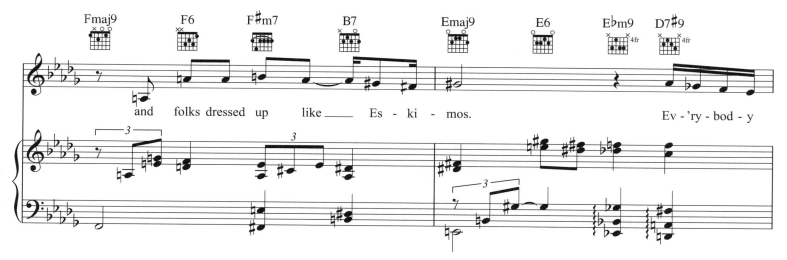

and folks dressed up like ___ Es - ki - mos. Ev - 'ry - bod - y

knows ___ a tur - key and ___ some mis - tle - toe ___

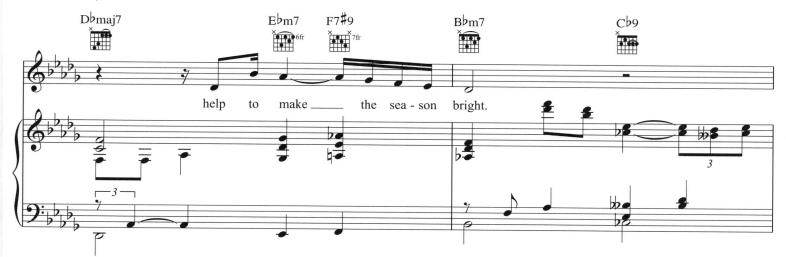

help to make ___ the sea - son bright.

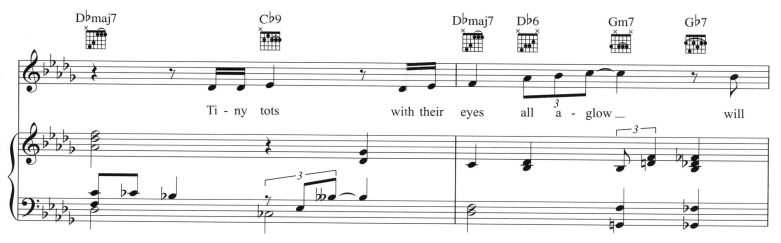

Ti - ny tots with their eyes all a - glow ___ will

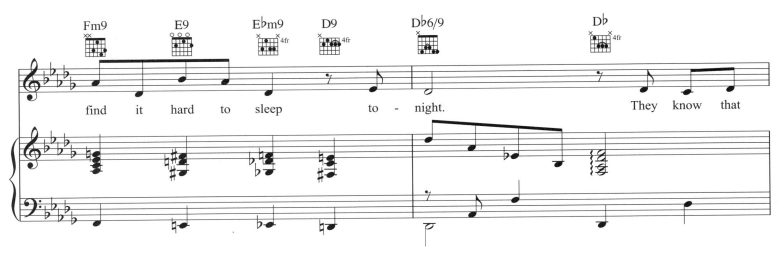

find it hard to sleep to - night. They know that

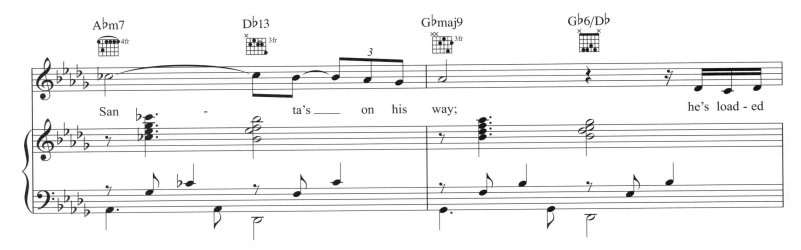

San - ta's ____ on his way; he's load - ed

lots of toys and good - ies _____ on his sleigh. And ev - 'ry

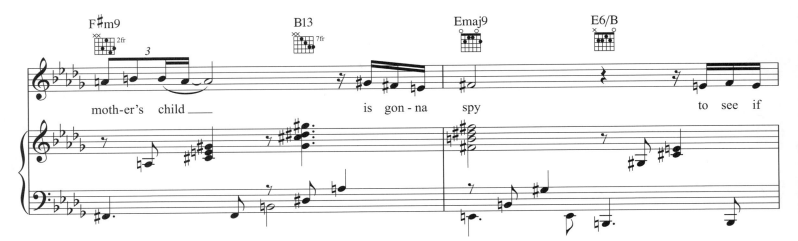

moth - er's child ____ is gon - na spy to see if

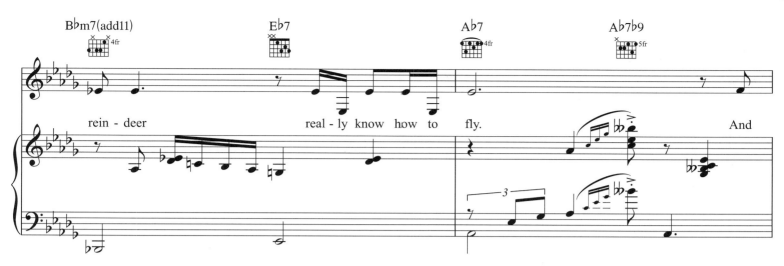

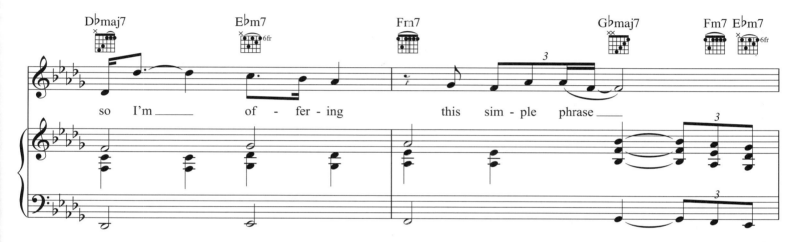

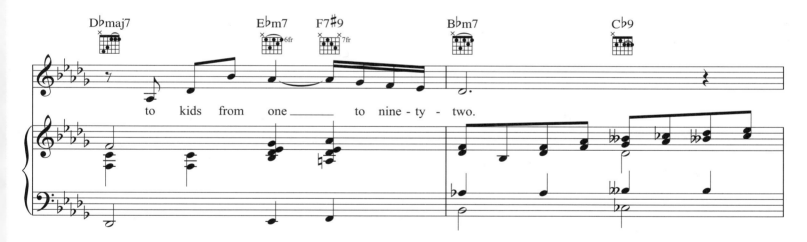

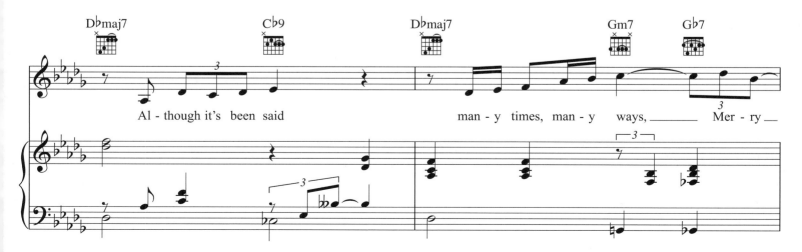

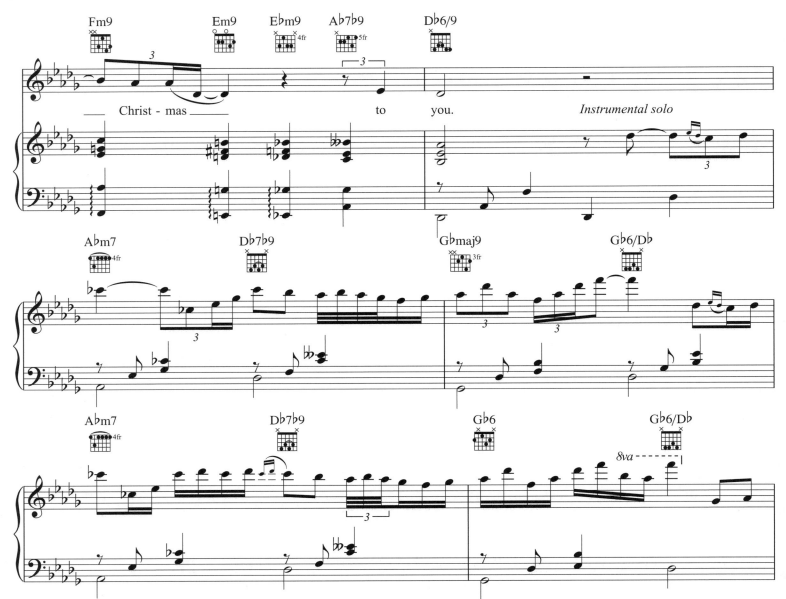

Christ - mas _____ to you. *Instrumental solo*

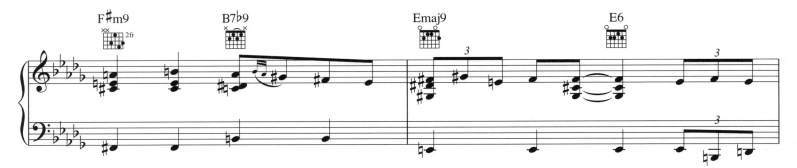

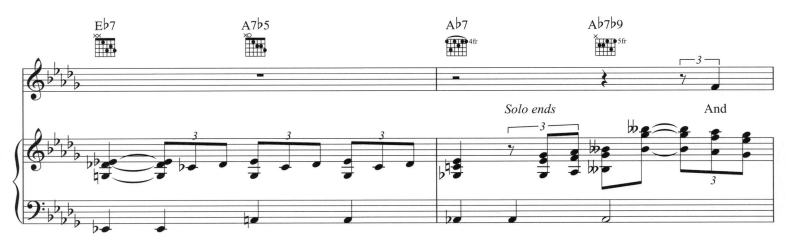

Solo ends And

GOD REST YE MERRY GENTLEMEN

Traditional
Arranged by PTX
and BEN BRAM

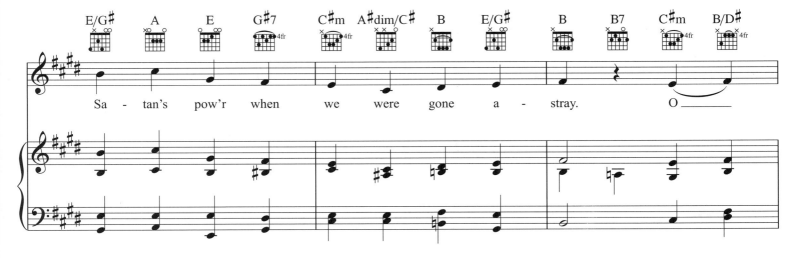

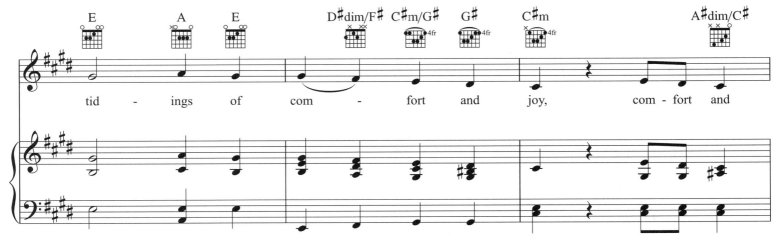

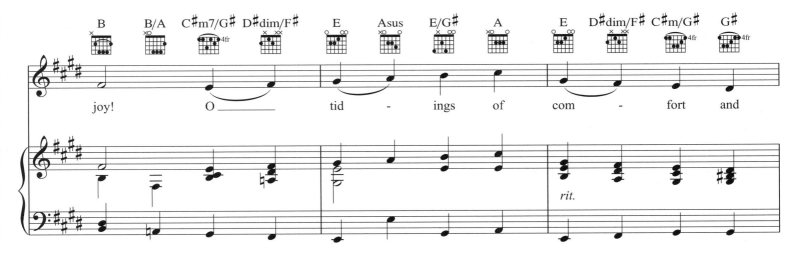

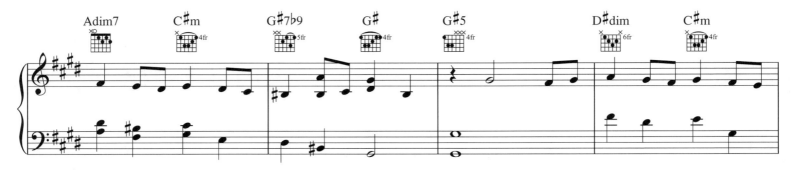

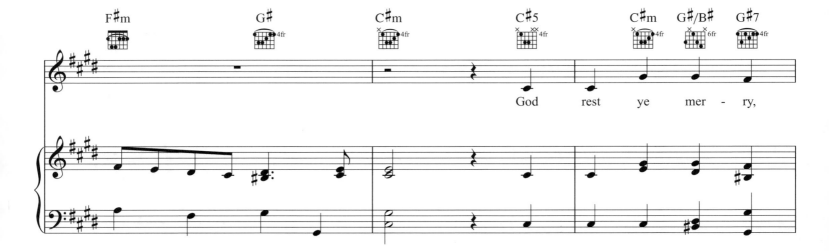

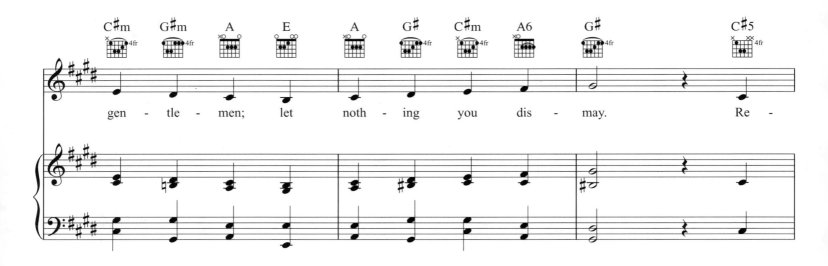

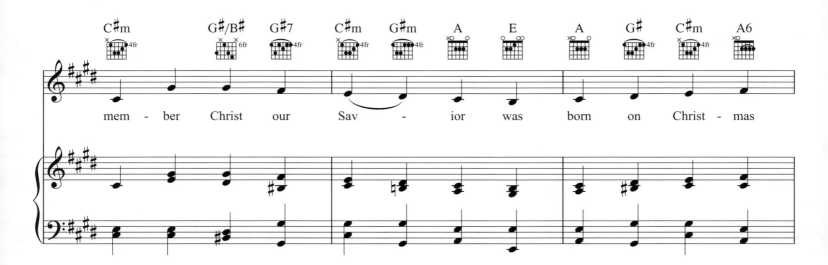

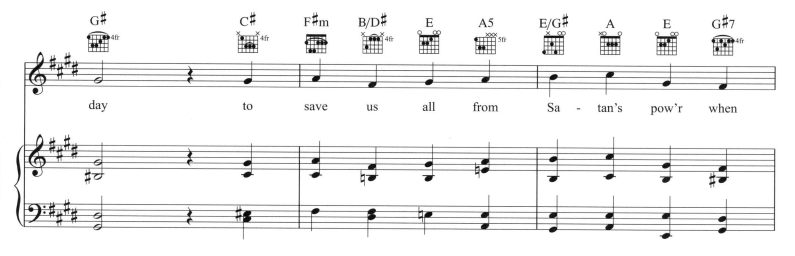

day to save us all from Sa - tan's pow'r when

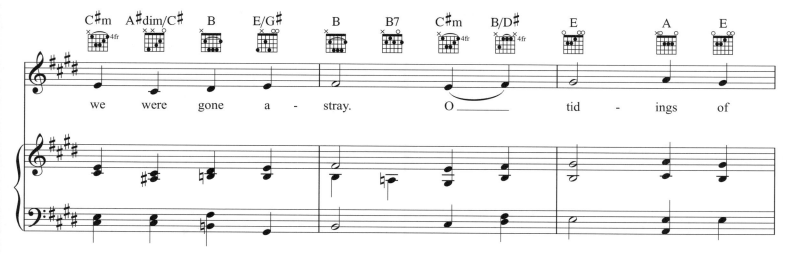

we were gone a - stray. O _____ tid - ings of

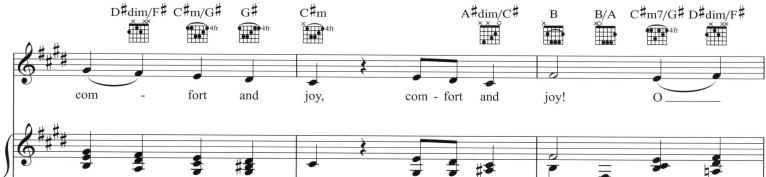

com - fort and joy, com - fort and joy! O _____

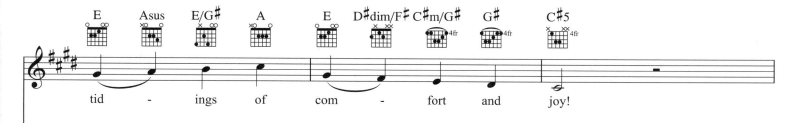

tid - ings of com - fort and joy!

78

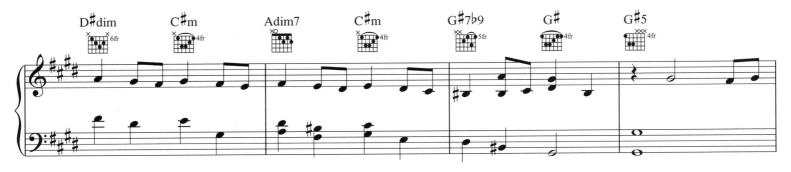

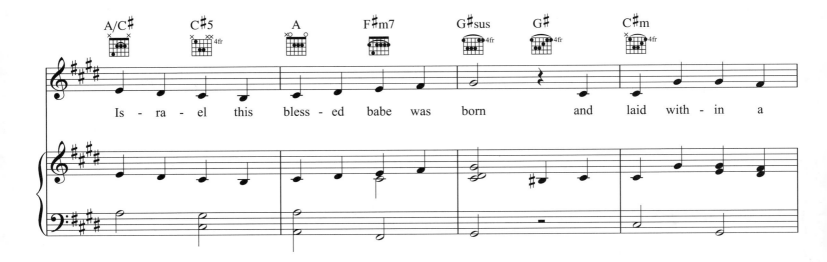

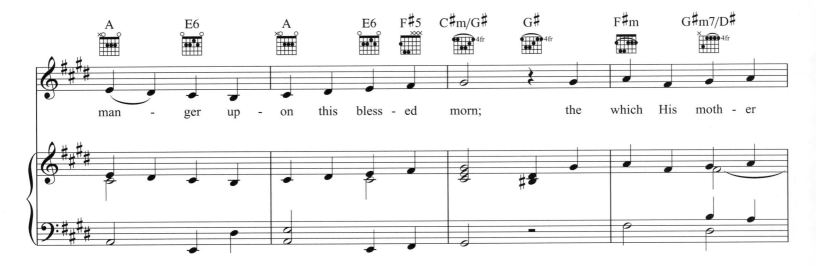

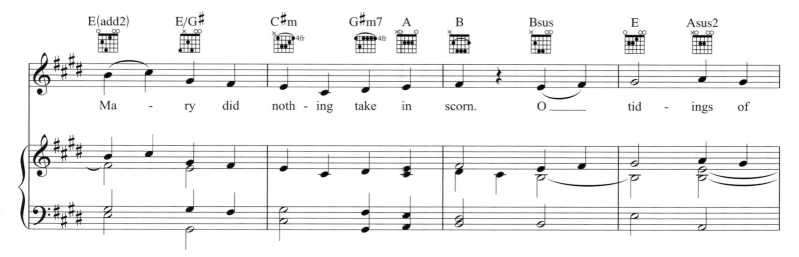

Ma - ry did noth - ing take in scorn. O _____ tid - ings of

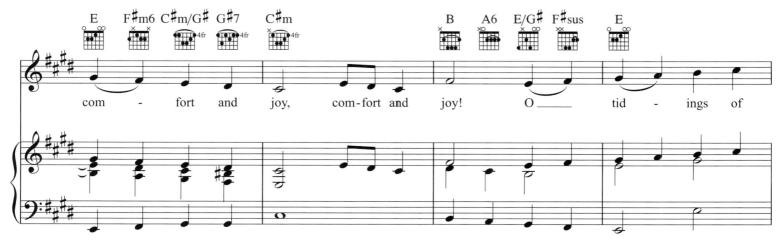

com - fort and joy, com-fort and joy! O _____ tid - ings of

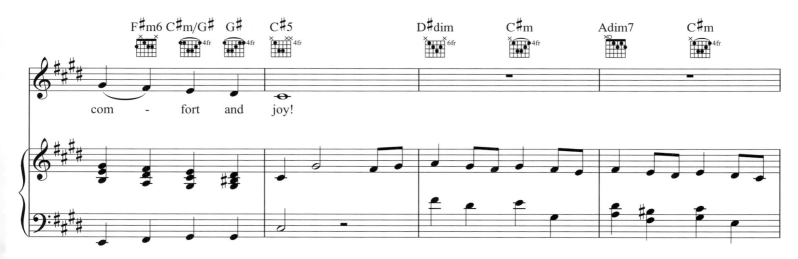

com - fort and joy!

"Fear

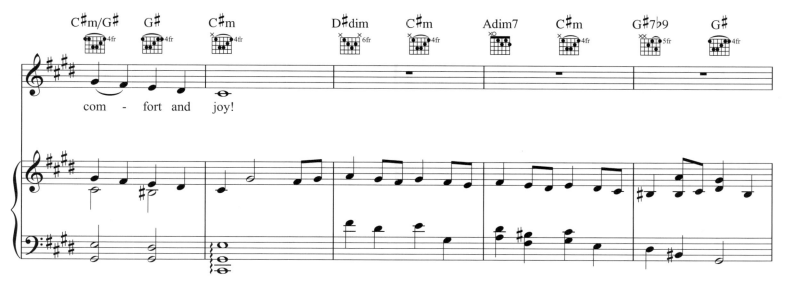

com - fort and joy!

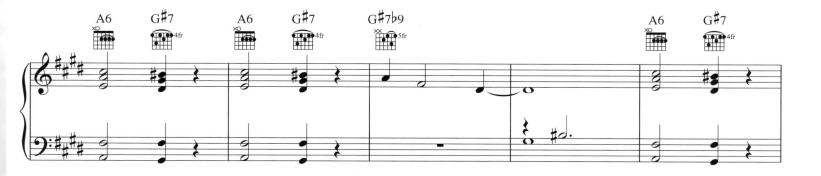

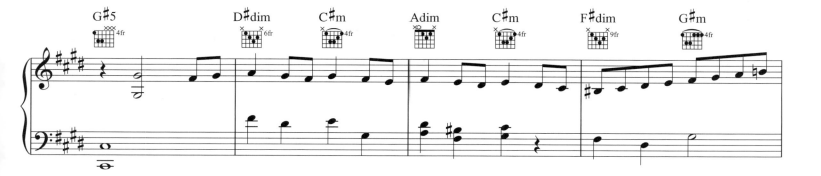

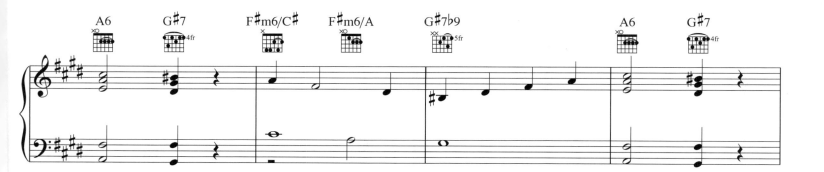

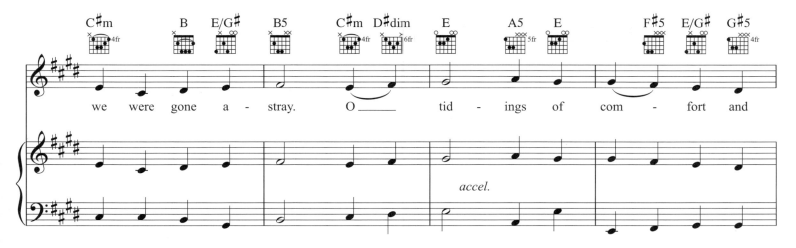

we were gone a - stray. O _____ tid - ings of com - fort and

accel.

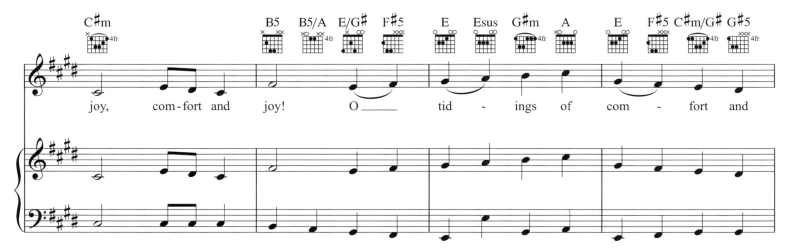

joy, com - fort and joy! O _____ tid - ings of com - fort and

Very fast

joy!

Hey!

A WONDERFUL AWFUL IDEA

By DANNY ELFMAN

Mysteriously

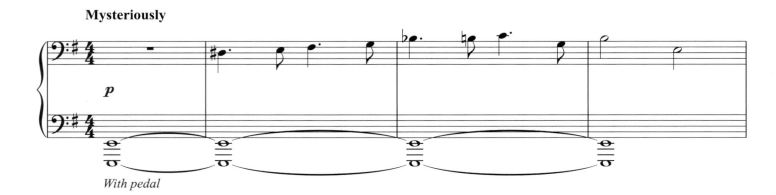

With pedal

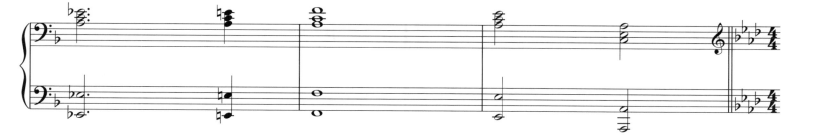

STEALING CHRISTMAS

By DANNY ELFMAN

Medium tempo

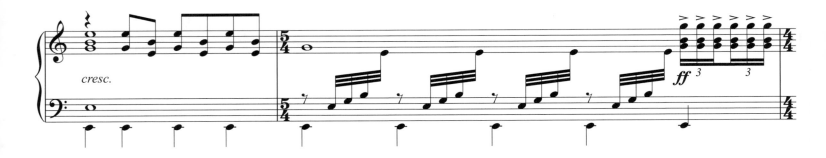

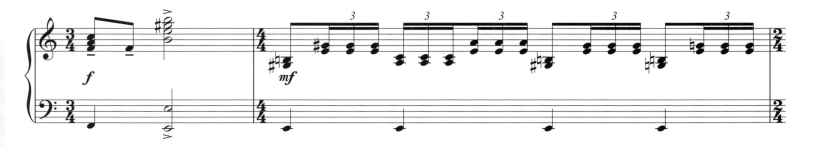

Hurrying

Slow